SERMON OUTLINES
on

First Corinthians

T0324270

Charles R. Wood

kregel
PUBLICATIONS

Grand Rapids, MI 49501

Sermon Outlines on First Corinthians

Copyright © 2006 by Charles R. Wood

Published in 2006 by Kregel Publications, a division of Kregel, Inc., P.O. Box 2607, Grand Rapids, MI 49501.

ISBN 0-8254-4142-0

Printed in the United States of America

1 2 3 4 5 / 10 09 08 07 06

Contents

Introduction

First is second, and second is fourth. Sound confusing? It is really very simple. Many Bible scholars are convinced from a careful study of the Corinthian letters that the letter we know as 1 Corinthians may well have been the second of four letters Paul wrote the church in that city. There is also much conjecture that the letter we know as 2 Corinthians is really the fourth of Paul's four letters.

If these speculations are correct, it is obvious that we have little or no information about the contents of the two "missing letters," which would lead a convinced biblicist to the conclusion that the missing information falls under the category of "things we don't really need to know." The volume of the material that we do have in the two extant books, however, is so great that it should obliterate any concern about what we don't know.

First Corinthians is really a "troubleshooter's toolbox," filled with detail about conditions in that church and Paul's responses to those troubling issues. Unfortunately, many of the same issues continue to plague the contemporary church. Fortunately, we have the inspired record of Paul's responses to guide us in our handling of troublesome situations.

The sermons in this book were preached to a local church congregation in consecutive order over a period of several months. They are uniformly backed by exegetical study and consultation with many commentators of the past and present. A deliberate attempt is made to get beneath the surface of many of the issues Paul addressed in Corinth to discover—and address—the real issues that underlay those that were apparent. The bias of the author is non-charismatic, but an attempt has been made to treat that tendency in such a way as to avoid offense.

The sermons may be treated as a series that covers the entire book, or they may be treated as individual messages on specific subjects. The outlines are not designed to be preached "as is," but rather to be organizing guidelines that set the stage for further research and development on the part of the individual preacher. May God bless to His church the uses made of this material. It is all His and to Him be any glory involved.

CHARLES R. WOOD

God's Epistle of Encouragement
Acts 18:1–18a

Introduction:
There is much talk about the irresistible force and an immovable object, regarding which would triumph in a direct confrontation. The question is somewhat moot because we have not developed perfection in either—it might be that both would just disintegrate. We have a story that touches on this question in Scripture, and that story forms the background for the book of 1 Corinthians.

I.   **The Irresistible Force: The Apostle Paul**
    A. He was God's man
    B. His character
        1. Morally pure
        2. Religiously just
        3. Personally self-controlled
        4. Naturally honest
        5. Certainly single-minded
    C. His program
        1. Spread the gospel
        2. Win converts
        3. Gather converts into churches

II. **The Immovable Object: The City of Corinth**
    A. Its culture was not as great as Athens but was still very great
        1. Known for beauty of art (Corinthian columns)
        2. Worldwide commercial center
        3. Highly intellectual society
    B. Its social structure
        1. A city of great wealth
        2. Wealth and slaves always went together at that time
        3. A melting pot for many peoples from diverse societies
    C. Its moral character
        1. Debased and depraved
        2. Its name was associated with vice—to "Corinthianize" was a "byword" for immoral conduct
        3. Reflected by Paul in Romans 1:18–32
        4. Called the "Paris of the ancient world"

D. Its religious nature
   1. A deeply religious city
   2. Its moral depravity was tied into its religious exercises
   3. Its religion approved moral depravity

III. **The Collision: What will happen when this irresistible force comes in contact with this immovable object?**
   A. The initial shock (vv. 1–6)
      1. Paul arrives and resides (vv. 1–5)
      2. He begins his ministry in the synagogue (v. 4)
      3. The coming of Silas and Timothy spur action (v. 5)
      4. The reaction is very violent (v. 6a)
      5. Paul pulls back (v. 6b); the immovable object has stood firm thus far
   B. The return engagement (vv. 7–8)
      1. Paul turns to the Gentiles (v. 7)
      2. He has some results (v. 8a)
      3. A church is established (v. 8b)
      4. He prepared to leave after indifferent results; the object and force seem to be at a standstill after this second encounter
   C. The final onslaught (vv. 9–18a)
      1. The vision from the Lord (vv. 9–10): "Do not fear to speak up and out because I am with you, and I have many people in the city that you don't know of yet" (author's paraphrase).
      2. The work progresses (v. 11)
      3. Opposition continues but fails (vv. 12–17)
      4. The city is impressed as a fine church is established
      5. The whole area was evangelized (2 Cor. 1:1) This time the irresistible force overcomes the immovable object

Conclusion:

There is only one irresistible force—the gospel. Never despair—there are many people in your city, community, and neighborhood who belong to the Lord. But don't resist—you will either yield to or be crushed by the judgment of God. Corinth couldn't resist; neither can you!

Cautions Concerning the Church of Jesus Christ
1 Corinthians

Introduction:
The church is always faced with problems and challenges. This is nowhere more evident than in Corinth. "Problem solving" is a primary purpose of both Corinthian letters.

I.   Divisions (1:10–17)

II.   The Pull of Intellectual Respectability (1:18–32)

III.   Carnality, Including the Exaltation of the Intellect (chap. 3)

IV.   Usurping the Role of Judge and the Place of Judgment (4:1–8)

V.   Misunderstanding the Ministry (4:9–21)

VI.   Toleration of Immorality (5:1–13)

VII.   A Litigious Attitude (6:1–18)

VIII. Immorality (6:19–20)

IX.   Marriage Problems (7:1–40)

X.   Abuse/Misuse of Liberty (chap. 8)

XI.   Neglect of God's Servants (chap. 9)

XII.   Worldliness (10:1–15)

XIII. Lack of Separation (10:16–22)

XIV.   Selfishness (10:23–33)

XV.   Exaltation of Experience (12:1–11)

XVI.   Failure to Recognize/Relate to the Body of Christ (12:12–31)

XVII. Lack of Love (chap. 13)

XVIII. Violation of Principles of Worship (chap. 14)

XIX.   Wrong Doctrine, Especially in Regard to the Resurrection) (chap. 15)

Conclusion:
The Corinthian church becomes a microcosm of the problems of churches today. Notice Paul corrects and enjoins correction rather than indicating a separation from or division in the church.

My Dear Corinthians
1 Corinthians 1:1–3

Introduction:

The opening portion of modern letters really doesn't mean much. The Greeks, however, were different. They put enough in the opening lines that one could tell a great deal about the letter from them. A case in point is 1 Corinthians.

I. **The Epistle's Authoritative Source (v. 1)**
   A. Declared—Paul
   B. Described—an apostle
      1. Means—"one sent"
      2. There was a special authority involved
         a. "Called . . . through the will of God." No human choice, personal or otherwise
         b. "Of Jesus Christ" indicates Christ's choice
      3. Why did he claim this?
         a. It had been questioned by false teachers
         b. It was needed to make his rebuke effective
         c. It was needed for authoritative answers to the questions submitted
   C. Demonstrated by the inclusion of Sosthenes
      1. He may have been the man in Acts 18:17
      2. This act showed Paul's basic humility and inclusive spirit

II. **The Epistle's Designated Destination (v. 2)**
   A. "The church of God at Corinth—take a look at that church
      1. Divided (1:10)
      2. Carnal (3:1)
      3. Critical (4:3)
      4. Containing undisciplined evil (5:1–2)
      5. Possessed of bad spirit (6:7)
      6. Morally evil (6:16)
      7. Disorderly in worship (11:17–21)
      8. Beginning to be infiltrated by doctrinal error (15:12)
   B. How can Paul even call it a church of God?
      1. Because it was made up of born-again people, the majority of whom still held to the truth
      2. Be careful of misunderstandings here. There are many groups today that are not churches at all even though they claim the title

C. The basic problem of this church
   1. Background
      a. "Sanctified in Christ Jesus" which means: "Set apart" at conversion and deals with position
      b. "Called saints"—along with all who call on the name of the Lord Jesus (actually means "called holy")
   2. Description
      a. Positionally—the Corinthians were set apart and holy
      b. Practically—they were just like all others and unholy
      c. Isn't this essentially the problem of the church today

III. **Its Dominant Design (v. 3): Having seen who the letter was from and to whom it was addressed, we now see . . .**
   A. The idea behind the greetings
      1. The normal, daily greetings of the time involved a wish
      2. For the Greeks—"grace"
      3. For the Hebrews—"peace"
   B. The meaning of the greetings translated into the Christian realm
      1. Grace—all good things from God
      2. Peace—the inner tranquility that comes from grace
      3. This is Paul's desire for Corinth
      4. Note the source of these—God and Christ

Conclusion:
Paul writes an authoritative letter of correction to a church that is living far below its position. He wished them grace and peace—and this is any good pastor's wish for his people. Paul's desire for the Christian was that position and practice would be the same. His desire for the unsaved was that they would come to know God's grace.

There's Always Something Good

1 Corinthians 1:4–9

Introduction:

I am always intrigued by chess and even more so by chess players who are always planning and thinking ahead. Intellectually organized people intrigue me, and Paul was one of them. He always had a plan, always knew what he was doing, even though sometimes it does not appear to be the case. This passage is an expression of thanksgiving, and it was planned and had a purpose.

I. **Its Stated Theme (v. 4)**
   A. Paul is always thankful concerning them. Whenever he prays, he thanks God for them
   B. The cause—the grace of God which is given them
      1. All the good favors of God
      2. "Given" is very important there—these are things not secured in any other way
   C. The limitation—by Jesus Christ
      1. Refers to those good things of God which come to us through Jesus Christ
      2. Distinguishes here between those who do and those who do not know Christ—the specific good things of God are available to believers alone

II. **Its Revealing Examination (vv. 5–9): Now we will take a look at this gift of grace as it relates to the Corinthian church**
   A. In the past (vv. 5–6)
      1. Examine the verb: should read "were" as it looks back, and it is a passive that indicates outside action
      2. Explore the meaning: "everything"—every spiritual area; "enriched"—made wealthy or opulent; "by Him"—it is the work of God
      3. Expand the areas in which it operates: all knowledge and utterance—the knowledge of spiritual things and the ability to express them
      4. Expose the source (v. 6)—the "testimony of Christ"—the gospel about Him; "was confirmed in you"—salvation; enrichment springs up as result of salvation

B. In the present (v. 7a) you do not "come behind"—you do not have to take second place
1. Having as much or more than anyone else does not come from any good in them
2. It does come from their enrichment by God
3. Salvation brings enrichment, and enrichment brings spiritual gifts
C. In the future (vv. 7b–9) "you are waiting"
1. Meaning: You are eagerly awaiting the second coming of Christ
2. Having the gifts makes one realize the imperfection of them, and the realization of their imperfection makes one want the completion of them in the second coming. In other words: salvation brings enrichment, enrichment brings gifts, and gifts make one want the consummation
3. Additional information (vv. 8–9)—God's grace not only makes you wait eagerly for the second coming, but promises to keep you until the second coming— note the teaching here:
a. He will confirm you to the end—means to speak for you until then, and God is faithful to take care of this
b. You were initially saved by God's call—not your own—and He will finish what He begins
c. You are in the fellowship—communion of Christ—this is a communion which you cannot break

III. Instructive Application
A. Note the emphasis in this thanksgiving
1. All this comes from God—"grace of God"
2. The emphasis is on Christ: nine mentions of Him in the first nine verses
3. There is not one thing here that the Corinthians could take personal credit for having achieved as Paul is honest and gives an accurate picture
B. Note the rebuke implied in this thanksgiving
1. They had been enriched—they let it puff them up and make spiritual treasure a matter of personal pride
2. They came behind no one in spiritual gifts, but they abused them to the point that Paul has to spend almost a quarter of his letter correcting the abuses

      3. They were waiting eagerly for the coming of the Lord—but they were not letting this have the purifying effect on them that it was designed to have

  C. Note the questions that this puts to us:
      1. We have been enriched—have we capitalized upon that enrichment, or have we allowed it to puff us up?
      2. We come behind in no spiritual gifts. Do we use them? Do we use them properly?
      3. We are looking for the Lord's return. Does the thought of this purify us?

Conclusion:

Even in this thanksgiving expression we hear the echo of the basic problems in the Corinthian church. They were not living up to what they actually were. Let us examine ourselves to see if we are really living as we ought to live.

Choosing Up Sides to Play Church
1 Corinthians 1:10–17

Introduction:
"The more things change, the more they stay the same." I don't know who said it, but I know it is true. First Corinthians is a book about church problems and lists at least twenty of them. Most of them are common to churches today. This passage contains much to be learned concerning them.

I. The Situation (vv. 11–12)
- A. Report from house of Chloe
- B. There is division (schism)
- C. Furthermore, there is contention arising out of division
- D. Nature of the divisions—they were following men, but division can be over other issues as well
  1. Paul: logical, intellectual
  2. Apollos: rhetorical, eloquent
  3. Peter: rough, straightforward
  4. Christ: "We don't bother with the teaching of mere men . . ."

II. The Stupidity (vv. 13–17)
- A. Obvious facts
  1. Christ is not divided
  2. Paul was not crucified for you
  3. There were no baptisms in the name of Paul
- B. Be careful of the situation on baptism
  1. This does not prove baptism unimportant or not present
  2. It surely does speak against baptismal regeneration
  3. It expresses Paul's commitments: primary—preach the gospel; result—baptize
  4. Likely others—Silas and Timothy—did the baptizing
- C. Shows
  1. Spiritual immaturity (carnality) [cf. 3:3–4]
  2. Lack of understanding [cf. 3:5–8] Christ and the gospel are the real issues

III. The Solution (v. 10)
- A. "I beseech"—appeal, beg
- B. Threefold request:
  1. All speak the same thing, agreeing on the essentials (a united testimony is in view)

2. There be no divisions: "Schisms, tears, cracks" ("maintain an unbroken front")
3. Be perfectly joined together: In mind and judgment (he desires inward harmony—not uniformity or unanimity but basic unity in the essentials of the faith)

Conclusion:

This is a strong appeal to the essential unity within a local church. As a result, we can structure some basic principles:

- Bible teachers have their place but the Word of God is the issue.
- You really can't know a Bible teacher like you can your own pastor.
- Some Bible teachers are probably such because they can't cut it as a pastor.
- Differences are properly resolved by carefully determining what one believes the Bible teaches rather than by simple acceptance of what someone else teaches.

Stick to the Basics

1 Corinthians 1:17–26

Introduction:
If evolution in its entirety is true, then it runs counter to virtually everything we know of science and life. We know that systems left to themselves tend to deteriorate so that they need intervention. Clocks run down without winding, and houses grow messier without cleaning. Commitments also run down over time, and Christian commitments are not an exception. It is obvious that this tendency to deteriorate was already a problem in Corinth.

I. **Natural Tendency**
   A. To change content of belief
      1. Salvation somehow without belief in finished work of Christ
      2. Theme of much teaching today
   B. To water down importance of essentials
      1. By becoming involved in social causes
      2. By allowing peripherals to become central
   C. To shift emphasis away from essentials
      1. Stress valid but nonessential aspects above their intrinsic worth
      2. Make evangelism secondary to something else

II. **Divine Treatment: Restatement of Facts**
   A. Our purpose (v. 17)
      1. Primary purpose
      2. Proclamation of good news
   B. Our power (v. 18)
      1. The message of the cross
      2. This is our only power (we are tempted to think otherwise)
   C. Our philosophy (vv. 19–22)
      1. God does everything His own way so as to bring glory to Himself
      2. He has chosen a particular way things should (must) be done
   D. Our passion (vv. 23–24)
      1. We proclaim Christ
      2. Proclamation has opposite effects; it turns off Jews and Greeks, but it becomes the power of God to those who respond to it

E. Our position (v. 25)
    1. God is wiser than men
    2. God has a way He wants things done
    3. We will do them God's way, or they won't get done

III. The Practical Teaching
A. Our problem
    1. Not changing the message—still hold there is no other way
    2. Not watering down the message—still stress faith alone, etc.
    3. Just a tendency to put it on the "back burner"
B. Our Process
    1. We have various issues to stress: education, edification, encouragement, etc.
    2. These matters tend to become primary
    3. All are outgrowths of evangelism, which is most important
C. Our priority
    1. Other things are important
    2. Evangelism must stay central
    3. It undergirds and is undergirded by all other things

Conclusion:
We need to take Paul to heart.
- Our purpose—proclaim the gospel
- Our power—the message of the cross
- Our philosophy—God's way is best
- Our passion—proclaim Christ
- Our position—do it God's way

Some say that our gospel is incomplete; some say that our gospel is inadequate. God says that the message of Christ crucified is complete and adequate—proclaim it, promote it, prioritize it.

Intellectual Respectability

1 Corinthians 1:26–2:16

Introduction:
If education is the answer, then what in the world is the question? We hear that:

- Education solves social problems.
- Education is necessary to success.
- Education is directly related to money-making ability.
- Education contributes to greater tolerance.
- Education engenders discernment
- Education makes one cultured.
- Education deals strictly with fact.

One need not be opposed to education to oppose the myths and exaggerated claims of education. There may be no premium on ignorance, but there is no biblical premium on intellect either. This is a very difficult passage, but there are three key verses in it.

I. **"That No Flesh Should Glory in His Presence" (1:29; see 1:26–31)**
   A. God's purpose—that all glory should be His (v. 29)
   B. God's procedure—select the lesser, etc. (vv. 27–28)
   C. God's proof—the experience of the church in Corinth (v. 26)
   D. God's provision—God gives us all the really important things so the glory will go to Him (vv. 30–31)

II. **"That Your Faith Should Not Stand in the Wisdom of Men, but in the Power of God" (2:5; see 2:1–5)**
   A. Paul's aim—to ground them in God in regard to their faith (v. 5)
   B. Paul's attitude—determined to keep the focus where it belongs—on Christ (v. 2)
   C. Paul's approach—came openly demonstrating his own weakness (vv. 1, 3–4)

III. **"That We Might Know the Things That Are Freely Given Us of God" (v. 12b; see 2:6–16)**
   A. The gifts
      1. The wisdom of God (v. 12a)
      2. The mind of Christ (v. 16)
      3. The deep things of God (vv. 9–12a)

B. The giving
1. Not given to unconverted (v. 14)
2. Given to us by the Spirit (vv. 10–13, etc.)

Conclusion:

So much has been lost in the quest for intellectual respectability! We have sometimes been sold a bill of goods about education and about who is best at educating. The church general and local has much to lose and nothing to gain from the enshrinement of human intellect.

Carnal Christians
1 Corinthians 3:1–23

Introduction:
Expatriates live in a foreign country and must determine which way they will lean culturally. This is very similar to the status of Christians in the world. Again, there are similar decisions that must be made.

I. **The Sickness**
   A. Carnality = worldliness
   B. What is worldliness?
      1. The usual definition: "things on list of do's and don'ts"
      2. It is really a matter of orientation: we live in two realms as expatriates, and worldliness is orientation to the old man/natural world
   C. Actually, worldliness is not a matter of the things we do or don't do. It is a philosophy, an orientation that causes us to do things, rather than the things themselves

II. **The Symptoms**
   A. Inability to handle differences in the church (v. 3)
      1. Material—jealousy
      2. Interpersonal strife
   B. It tends to take two forms
      1. Preferring men (vv. 4–8): either one man over another, or a man over the Word
      2. The most common form, however, is to shop for opinions rather than dig in the Word
   C. Building with wrong materials (vv. 9–15)
      1. Note various ingredients
         a. Gold, etc., spiritual things
         b. Wood, etc., worldly things
      2. Likely deals with
         a. Biblical reality versus worldly unreality
         b. A matter of motives
   D. Failure to appreciate the Holy Spirit (vv. 16–17)
      1. This passage has reference to church
      2. We need to take great care in the church regarding these things
   E. Confidence in human wisdom (vv. 18–23)
      1. Setting personal opinions before God's
      2. Accepting the world's wisdom over God's

III. The Source
   A. Which came first, our biblical ignorance or our shallowness? (vv. 1–2)
   B. The truth is that we are worldly because we are biblically shallow, and we are biblically shallow because we are worldly
   C. The answer lies in a decision of the will to orient in one direction or the other

IV. The Solution
   A. A decision of the will
      1. We live in two societies
      2. We mush decide which one will dominate
   B. This is what 1 John 2:15 means

Conclusion:
All of us are worldly in some ways in that we aren't exactly sure of our orientation. Have you determined which way you are going to lean and live? Carnality (worldliness) is a problem of major proportion in today's church. Are you part of the problem or are you part of the solution?

Get Off the Throne

1 Corinthians 4:1–8

Introduction:

We are told in Scripture to discern ("to tell the difference between"), but we are forbidden to judge ("determine the reasons why"). Unfortunately, we often do poorly at what we are required to do and do well at what we are forbidden to do.

I. **A Significant Difference**
   A. We are commanded to be discerning: to make differences on the basis of objective and visible evidence (1 Cor. 2:14; 12:10)
   B. We are forbidden to judge: to form opinions about, to criticize, censure (Matt. 7:1–2; Luke 6:37; Rom. 14:10, 13)

II. **A Clear Command**
   A. Simply stated—"judge nothing"
   B. Has to do with passing judgment on invisible or non-objective matters
   C. In short—stay off the throne and the bench

III. **A List of Reasons**
   A. Because other men ultimately are solely accountable to God (v. 1)
      1. Paul sees himself thus
      2. He was a servant belonging to Christ who had been given his ministry
   B. Because we use incorrect criteria (v. 2)
      1. Faithfulness is the prime criteria
      2. We tend to use various others
   C. Because we can't judge ourselves (vv. 3–4)
      1. Christ is Lord of conscience; only He can judge it justly
      2. A clear conscience is significant but not finally determinative
   D. Because there is an appointed time of judgment coming (v. 5b)
      1. God will judge unseen things
      2. There is a proper time and place for this
      3. Our judgment usurps God's throne
   E. Because only God can know the things that we can't (v. 5c)
      1. He will expose what is hidden in the darkness
      2. This is basically the motives, etc., of the human heart

F. Because we don't qualify as judges (vv. 6–8)
    1. We don't understand necessary factors
    2. We don't have the necessary wisdom
    3. We uniformly do a poor job

Conclusion:

We need ever more discernment, but we need far less judgment. We can't know what others think, etc., so we would do well to talk less. We need to identify judgments as such and leave them alone. Are you doing poorly at what you should do? Are you doing well at what you are forbidden to do?

Misunderstanding Your Minister

1 Corinthians 4:9–21

Introduction:

Sometimes a pastor is misunderstood in communication, but that isn't a major issue. Often a pastor is misunderstood in ministry. People infer wrong motives, etc., and this does become an issue. Paul faced the same situations and gave guidelines for handling them.

I. **Paul's Analysis**
   A. The way he felt (v. 9)
      1. Emphasis on being made to feel like a "spectacle"
      2. Sometimes we feel that way—singled out by God for abuse
   B. The way the Corinthians saw it (v. 10)
      1. They saw themselves as wiser, etc.
      2. This is like trying to convince some people to listen
   C. The way things looked (vv. 11–13)
      1. There always are "outward appearances"
      2. They made it look like the first two observations were correct
   D. The way it really was (vv. 14–15)
      1. There were many people saying many things
      2. But he was their "father" in the sense of birth and long-term care

II. **Paul's Appeal (vv. 16–17)**
   A. Stated: "Be ye followers of me"
      1. This is a conditional statement (see 1 Cor. 11:1)
      2. Anyone who walks with the Lord can actually say the same thing
   B. Supported: "I have sent Timothy"
      1. He will remind you of my ways
      2. My ways are both "In Christ" and the same everywhere I minister

III. **Paul's Accusation (vv. 18–21)**
   A. Some say I am weak
   B. We will find out who is weak
      1. Talk is cheap, but power is obvious
      2. "If you are so smart, why aren't you rich?" A stinging rebuke to a very mixed-up church

Conclusion:

We all evaluate preaching, and we do so all the time. It is not wrong to do so, but we must use proper criteria. Usually, we use the idea of agreement, but this is wrong. In reality, agreement with the preacher is inconsequential. Our concern should be whether or not the preacher agrees with the Word. If he does, and your are resisting the message, you are judging God's Word. The only way to know for sure is from Scripture. Be careful that you don't fall into the trap of thinking all is well because you agree or disagree with a preacher.

An Unleavened Church
1 Corinthians 5

Introduction:
Preaching through 1 Corinthians is not always easy because the book is a compendium of church problems, and many of those same problems exist today. Prior to reaching chapter 5, Paul has addressed divisions, a tendency to "water down" the message, the question of intellectual respectability, carnality, judging rather than discerning, and misunderstanding the ministry. Chapter 5 has more to offer in the way of problems.

I. **The Theme Involved (vv. 6–8)**
   A. Identified: Failure to deal with impurity in the church
   B. Stated:
      1. Evil tends to permeate (v. 6)
      2. Permeating evil must be removed for the good of the body (v. 7)
   C. Reasoned:
      1. Christ has died for us
      2. We should be pure as a result (probably Paul was writing around Passover time)

II. **Group Action (vv. 1–4)**
   A. The problem: sin that was
      1. Public
      2. Pernicious
      3. Proud
   B. The prescription
      1. Put him out
      2. Explain "deliver to Satan" (1 Tim. 1:20). Probably means to withdraw the safeguards that were provided by being part of the "household of faith" in a local church so that Satan would have easier access to the person
   C. The process
      1. Act with great care
      2. Be sure of the spiritual basis for any action
   D. The purpose
      1. Purity
      2. Correction
      3. Reconciliation

III. Individual Action (vv. 9–13)
A. The rule: Don't associate with the immoral
B. The exception
   1. Obviously does not include unsaved people (this thought may have been used as an argument against what Paul was promoting)
   2. Be careful of imposing Christian standards on unsaved people
C. The intention
   1. Don't associate with a disorderly brother regardless of church action
   2. Involves a measure of discernment and somewhat points up our wrong reasons for friendships, etc.
   3. Such action involves strong commitment to the authority of the Word and the welfare of the individual. (We sometimes say, "Somebody's got to love them," but that depends on the meaning of love.)

Conclusion:

Don't worry about people on the outside; deal with those on the inside. God will take care of the unsaved world. He has entrusted to you the care of the church. Take appropriate action (don't wait for the church to act if you see wrong that is provable).

The Court of Last Resort

1 Corinthians 6:1–8

Introduction:

Sometimes an apparent problem covers many more problems. Sometimes an apparent problem covers a real problem. The surface problem here is serious, but the worst part is that it covers other problems and disguises the real problem.

I. **The Apparent Problem (v. 1)**
    A. Stated: believers going to law before unbelievers
    B. Explained
        1. Has to do with civil matters (exempts criminal or legal matters)
        2. This is an appeal not a command (this fact may leave the door open in certain situations)
        3. It does not relate to unbelievers or to situations that involve unbelievers. The church has no control over them

II. **Additional Problems (vv. 2–8): An Apparent Problem Covers Other Problems**
    A. A wrong view of the church (vv. 2–3)
        1. God trusts saints more than saints trust saints
        2. Saints are special—will judge mankind and angels
        3. Christians don't usually trust the church structure for solving problems
    B. Wrong attitude (v. 4)
        1. The things Paul is speaking of could be judged by the least in the church
        2. This demonstrates their relative importance
        3. They were making the unimportant greatly important
    C. Wrong approach (v. 5)
        1. Are there no wise among you?
        2. Are all the wise in the world?
        3. God says, "I'm smarter than the world . . ."
    D. Wrong values (v. 6)
        1. Going to law before unbelievers
        2. Results in showing our problems, admitting our incompetence, and compromising our beliefs before the unsaved world
        3. What about the bad testimony involved?

29

E. Wrong spirit (v. 7)
  1. Is it really necessary to pursue this issue?
  2. Subsidiary questions: Why not be like Christ? Are these things really that important?
  3. Your problem: you are all tied up in your own "rights"
F. Wrong actions (v. 8)
  1. You do the kinds of things that result in going to law
  2. It's bad to do these things—matters such as sins against trust or sins against the body—and worse to do them to brethren

III. **Actual Problem: The Apparent Problem Is Not the Real Problem**
  A. The real problem was materialistic humanism or humanistic materialism
    1. Materialism: preoccupation with possession, ownership, rights
    2. Humanism: preoccupation with appearances and human wisdom
  B. Going to law showed something wrong underneath
  C. They needed to deal with the real problem

Conclusion:
We've learned not to go to court with fellow believers. But have we learned to deal with the real problems that drive us to court—our low view of the church and of its ability to deal with problems? We have a materialistic mentality that makes *things* more important than anything, and our humanism places unlimited faith in human wisdom. If we would make the local church the court of last resort, we might be too embarrassed to pursue our materialism and humanism, which are our real problems.

Questions on the Christian Life
1 Corinthians 7

Introduction:

Some believe that the King James translators were biased regarding marriage (they may have been), and that their bias shows in this chapter. That is highly unlikely. What we really see in this chapter is an attempt on the part of Paul to answer some questions regarding marriage, the single life, etc.

I.   **Must a Christian Marry? (vv. 1–2, 7–9, 25–38)**
    A.   It is not necessary, but it is normal (vv. 1–2)
    B.   Exception: the gift of celibacy (vv. 7–9)
        1.   Those who have it should exercise it
        2.   Those who don't, shouldn't
    C.   What about the unmarried woman? (vv. 15–38)
        1.   Her source of authority (v. 25)
        2.   The general rule (v. 26–28)
        3.   Some priority considerations (vv. 29–35)
            a.   Perspective (vv. 29–31)
            b.   Practicalities (vv. 32–35)
        4.   The father of the non-bride is also mentioned (vv. 36–38)

II.   **How About "Christian Celibacy"? (vv. 3–6)**
    A.   The problem—the crisis in the Roman Catholic Church of sexual crimes stems at least partly from a misunderstanding of biblical celibacy
    B.   The correction
        1.   Mutual obligation (v. 3)
        2.   Mutual surrender of rights (v. 4)
        3.   Highly limited restraints (v. 5)
        4.   Qualified instruction (v. 6)
    C.   Further implications
        1.   The sexual side of marriage proper
        2.   There is a total commitment in marriage

III. **What About Divorce? (vv. 10–11)**
    A.   Prohibition
    B.   Purpose—should never be with thought of remarriage already in mind
    C.   Practicalities

IV.   **How About Mixed Marriages? (vv. 12–16)**
    A.   It was an early church problem

B. "If it ain't broke . . ." (vv. 12–14)
C. "So long, it's been good to know you" (v. 15)
D. Leave it to God (v. 16)

V. Should Salvation Change One's Marital Status? (vv. 17–24)
A. Suggested by marriage considerations
B. Principles (vv. 17, 20, 24)
C. Explanations
  1. Religious background immaterial (vv. 18–19)
  2. Social status immaterial (vv. 21–23; note caution of v. 23)

VI. How Does Death Affect Marriage? (vv. 39–40)
A. Death frees survivor
B. Freedom is complete
C. Remarriage questions (v. 40)

Conclusion:
Early days of Christianity raised many questions about marital relationships. We can only conjecture about some of them. Those raised here are answered by the text. A brief summary:

- Must a Christian marry? It is normal but not necessary (especially if God has given the spiritual gift of celibacy).
- How about Christian celibacy? It is wrong except under the most limited conditions.
- How about divorce? It is not a viable option for a Christian except under certain very specific conditions.
- How about mixed marriages? Stay with them if at all possible but don't keep them at any price.
- Does salvation change marital status? Normally speaking, no.
- What is the effect of death on marriage? It severs any and all bonds.

The Misuse of Christian Liberty
1 Corinthians 8:1–13

Introduction:

On some issues Scripture is very clear (e.g., adultery, lying, stealing, etc.). In many other areas, however, it is silent (e.g., movies, smoking, the draft, roller skating, etc.). In the areas where it is silent, Scripture does lay down some applicable principles.

I. **Problem Revealed (v. 1a)**
  - A. Specific form—things offered to idols
    1. Explain peculiar religious situation
    2. The association of the meat with idol worship raised questions
  - B. Issues involved
    1. The meat itself was morally neutral
    2. Because of wrong use, a question arises about the Christian's relationship to it
  - C. Modern applications
    1. Things neutral in themselves are frequently put to improper use
    2. What about the Christian's relationship to them?

II. **Proposed Solution (vv. 1b, 4–6, 8)**
  - A. We have knowledge (v. 1b)
    1. As Christians were are enlightened
    2. The more mature the Christian, the more enlightened he should be
  - B. We can apply this knowledge (vv. 4–6)
    1. We know that an idol is not a god
    2. We know there is only one God
    3. Therefore, things offered to idols are really offered to nothing and are therefore clean up to this point
  - C. We are secure in this knowledge (v. 8)
    1. Our relationship to God does not depend on what we eat or do not eat
    2. On the basis of this solution, we would say that there is no reason at all why one shouldn't eat idol meat

III. **Proffered Alternative (vv. 1c–3, 7, 9–12)**
  - A. The entrance of another dimension—love (vv. 1–3)
    1. It is contrasted with knowledge
    2. It is shown to be superior to knowledge

B. The problem of knowledge pointed out (v. 7)
  1. Not everyone has developed knowledge
  2. Some will still see something valid in the whole matter and be harmed by eating idol meat (they may even be drawn back into idolatry)
C. The role played by love (vv. 9–12)
  1. The one who loves judges his liberty by the effects it may have on others, particularly the weak
    a. The weak see you indulge and are emboldened to indulge also
    b. In the process the weak are harmed by such indulgence
    c. Thus the one who leads astray sins against the weak and also against Christ
  2. Therefore the principle of love will cause the really mature to forgo any questionable practice that may harm someone who is weaker

IV. Positive Application

A. Transfer of teaching
  1. Idol meat is no problem today
  2. The applications are both broad and obvious
B. Where Scripture is silent on specifics, it does speak principles
  1. Some things are specifically mentioned as right or wrong—no problem here
  2. Some things, although not mentioned by name, come under principles such as not defiling the Holy Ghost's temple
  3. Things still not covered but generally considered to be doubtful must be considered in the light of their effects on others
C. Are there no limitations on the weaker brother?
  1. This principle can be misused so as to allow one who claims weakness to dictate another's conduct
  2. Question: Who is really a weaker brother? A young person, a younger Christian, or a person with a genuine conscience problem in a particular area

Conclusion:

Whenever we spend all of our time arguing about do's and don'ts, we end up ignoring weightier principles. Are we willing to submit our "liberty" to the examination of this chapter?

A Little Self-Defense Is in Order

1 Corinthians 9:1–27

Introduction:

There were so many questions about Paul in Corinth. It seems as if he was always under attack from some quarter. If it wasn't one thing, it was another. This passage contains an interesting defense against some of the attacks.

I. **He Proves His Apostleship (9:1–2)**
   A. Requisite—seeing the Lord
      1. Paul had done this
      2. Apostolic office does not continue because no one living has seen the Lord
   B. Lord had granted him special appearances (Acts 22:14; 26:14–16; 1 Cor. 15:8)
   C. Questions came from Paul's occasional failure to act on all his apostolic rights
   D. He enumerates all his reasons for not doing so (9:1–2)
      1. He does have a "claim to fame"—the souls he had won
      2. They of all people should know

II. **He Shows That He Has the Same Rights as Others (9:3–6)**
   A. "Power" means "right"
   B. He had a right to proper support
   C. The fact that he was unmarried raised some questions (and the mention here raises questions about celibacy today)
   D. The fact that he worked with his hands was also used as an argument against him
      1. He said that he had a right to support
      2. Paul may have had a little trace of pride at this point

III. **He Proves the Rights That Were His (9:7–14)**
   A. Illustrations—appropriate for ministry (v. 7)
      1. No one fights for the fun of it
      2. No one plants a vineyard for the fun of it
      3. The shepherd has a right to the fruit of the flocks
   B. The teaching of the law (vv. 8–10)
      1. Right to support is in accord to the principles of the Old Testament
      2. Oxen are cared for on this score—not preachers
      3. The work is properly done in view of a reward to be granted

C. The logic of good thinking
    1. Aren't the spiritual things worth something? (v. 11)
    2. The fact that we haven't exercised this right doesn't alter its truth (v. 12)
D. The example of the Old Testament priests (v. 13)
E. The principle stated (v. 14)
    1. "Ordained"—the Lord's will
    2. Living should be provided (this is a good section on why we have paid clergy)

IV. **He Gives Reasons for Not Taking Advantage of His Rights (9:15–27)**
A. Paul felt this was the best way for him
B. He wanted to keep service on a fully voluntary basis (vv. 16–19)
    1. This would lead to great reward
    2. This is a tremendous demonstration of proper attitude
C. He makes accommodations as far as possible and consistent with good principle for the purpose of the gospel (vv. 20–23)
D. He states clearly his ultimate purpose (vv. 24–27)
    1. The absolute supremacy of the gospel
    2. The totality of his focus in that area

Conclusion:

This is a section that is very technical and specific, but it provides a beautiful display of the proper attitude in service. How wonderful it would be if the gospel could be this important to us! Most of us aren't interested in even being inconvenienced by the spread of the gospel.

Idling with Immorality

1 Corinthians 8:9–20

Introduction:

All sin is sin, but the Bible seems to view some sins as more serious than others. Two that stand out appear to be murder, because it usurps the authority of God, and immorality, because it goes against the character of God. Paul has immorality in view in this section, and he gives five reasons why it is wrong.

I. **Because It Confuses Our Identity (vv. 9–11)**
   A. It reveals the absence of the changes that accompany salvation
   B. It identifies us with the wrong crowd
   C. It misunderstands the work of conversion
      1. You were such "things"
      2. But what has happened? You are washed, sanctified, and justified

II. **Because It Violates God's Order (v. 12)**
   A. We may not always be able completely to control our emotions
   B. We are responsible to control our actions
   C. Immorality is really emotions controlling actions

III. **Because It Defies God's Purposes (vv. 13–17)**
   A. God's purpose for the body
      1. It is temporary
      2. It is to be used for God's glory. We are more than responders to the animal impulse (this is a gnawing issue that surfaces in much support for abortion)
      3. It belongs to Christ
   B. Immorality results in a union of bodies
      1. "He who joins himself" (v. 16)
      2. This brings Christ into a wrong relationship
   C. Immorality creates a contradiction
      1. What belongs to Christ is offered to another
      2. The biblical picture is thus messed up

IV. **Because It Is Sin Against One's Body (v. 18)**
   A. Immorality involves the body—most sin doesn't
   B. This raises questions about our selves
      1. Self-respect
      2. Ability to keep a covenant
      3. Self-control

C. Flee—keep on fleeing—immorality. Fight some things; flee immorality

V. Because It Misunderstands the Body's Role (vv. 19–20)
A. The Holy Spirit dwells in us
B. We are not our own
1. Final determination of what we do with our body is not ours
2. This fact changes all relationships/concepts
C. The body should be used to glorify God

Conclusion:

There are two key directions here: (1) "keep on fleeing fornication" and (2) "glorify God in your body." Immorality is worse than many other sins, which is why we are commanded not even to think about it. It is so important that we teach our children to avoid it. Yes, it is difficult, but it was very difficult then as there were no laws whatsoever regarding it. Regardless, the commandments of God's Word never depend on the standards of any contemporary society. We need to make some heart commitments and then keep on fleeing.

The War Against the World
1 Corinthians 10:1–14

Introduction:
What is worldliness? Is it short skirts and long hair? Going to movies and playing cards? Wearing makeup and having bobbed hair? Having nice clothes, a fancy car, and a big house? There is really no agreement on these and similar matters. Actually, worldliness is a good deal more than this. Paul deals with the subject, and in the process provides a definition.

I. **Comparison (vv. 1–5)**
    A. Israel had great blessing—they had God's
        1. Guidance
        2. Protection
        3. Identification
        4. Provision relationship
    B. Note the "many" (most) (v. 5)

II. **Catalogue (vv. 6–10)**
    A. They had so many blessings that they were almost innumerable
    B. With all the blessing, however, they did wrong
        1. Lusted after evil things (i.e., has to do with inordinate desire; Num. 11:4, 31–34)
        2. Became idolaters (Exod. 32:1–6)
        3. Committed fornication (Num. 25:1–9)
        4. Tried God (i.e., to try His patience, try to see how much He will put up with—they did so by rebellion, murmuring, impatience, dissatisfaction, etc.; Num. 21:5–6)

III. **Contrast (v. 11)**
    A. These things are examples to us (cf. v. 6)
        1. That we should not desire what is not rightfully ours
        2. That we should not become idolaters (has to do with anything that is valued or worshiped above God)
        3. That we should not become immoral (in thought or deed)
        4. That we should not put God to the test
        5. That we should not grumble, complain

B. We have the same—and greater—blessing of God and thus the same tendency to failure. This is the essence of worldliness
   1. Wanting what I don't have
   2. Wanting what I don't need
   3. Wanting what God doesn't want me to have
   4. Wanting something, anything because I am not satisfied with God and with what He has given me. (I won't put something ahead of Him unless I am not satisfied with Him)

IV. Cautions (vv. 12–14)
   A. Against self-confidence (v. 12)
   B. Against defeat/despair (v. 13)
   C. Against passivity (v. 14)
      1. Don't just sit there! Do something
      2. Flee from all idolatry and everything that might lead in that direction

Conclusion:

Find your satisfaction in God and in what He gives you. Worldliness is not dress, hair, possessions, or practices. It is rather an attitude of dis- or un-satisfaction with or in Christ. That attitude will show itself in external ways, but it is not the externals. Worldliness is an attitude that is not fulfilled by the blessings of God and, thus, goes after fulfillment in other places or tries God or murmurs against God.

Separating the "Tacky Stuff"
1 Corinthians 10:16–11:1

Introduction:
So many practical questions confront us. Your nephew is marrying a Catholic girl. Should you attend the wedding? Your pastor is invited to speak at a liberal church. Should he accept the invitation? Your neighbor's son is confirmed, and you are invited to a luncheon honoring him. Should you attend? Your recently saved stepfather dies. The rest of the family wants a Masonic service. What should you do? In brief, what do you do with the "tacky stuff"? Here are some principles from Paul.

I. **A Basic Principle (10:16–22)**
    A. The argument
        1. Communion identifies us with Christ
        2. Partaking of sacrifices identifies Jews with Judaism
    B. The statement: participating in rites identifies us with the religion
    C. We cannot identify with Christianity and non-Christianity at the same time
    D. Summary: dealing here with the principle of identification

II. **Some Basic Perimeters (10:23–24, 31–33): Principle of identification needs boundaries. Whole idea of limitations on liberty enters in here also**
    A. The rule of self-denial (v. 23)
    B. The rule of preference for others (v. 24)
    C. The rule of ultimate purpose (v. 31)
    D. The rule of non-offense (vv. 32–33)

III. **Some Practical Applications (10:25–11:1)**
    A. Don't worry about food in the market—it all comes from God anyhow (vv. 25–26)
    B. Don't ask about what is set before you (v. 27)
    C. Don't eat what you know was offered to idols (vv. 28–30)

Conclusion:
General rules:
- If you don't know, don't worry.
- If you do know, don't do it.
- If someone raises an issue, don't do it even if you know it doesn't matter.

Disorderly Conduct
1 Corinthians 11:2–16

Introduction:

Some believe that women must wear a hat in church or that a woman must never cut her hair. Both of those beliefs are based on this passage which is admittedly extremely difficult to interpret. Settling for a discussion of such questions, however, misses the point of the passage. There is something far more basic here. We need to begin with Romans 12:2: "Don't let the world around you squeeze you into its mold" (author's paraphrase).

I. **The Role of Culture/Custom**
   A. Not all custom is wrong. Custom comes in three forms: good, neutral, and wrong
   B. Origination of custom
      1. Some arises directly out of general/special revelation
      2. Some grows up because it works
      3. Some comes through rebellion against other traditions and customs
   C. Criteria for discernment
      1. Does it conform to the Word?
      2. What is its historic significance?
      3. What is the relative age of its emphasis?
      4. What is the character of those who promote it?
      5. What are the reasons given for its promotion?

II. **The Assault of Culture**
   A. Rebellious custom assails the church
      1. Men hate God (i.e., evil deeds)
      2. They thus seek to overthrow His dominion
      3. They thus turn on His visible church
   B. Particular instance—radical feminism
      1. Their ultimate good is absolute equality
      2. They think a woman must be free to perform all functions of man
      3. Anything less than equality is inferiority even though the concepts are not opposite
   C. Check the criteria for feminism
      1. It arises out of a rebel view
      2. It should be resisted but is being accepted

III. **The Answer to Culture**
   A. The problem in Corinth
      1. Women were getting out of hand in worship
      2. Women were praying/prophesying with heads uncovered (vv. 4–6)
      3. This was a general problem of disrespect in the culture of that time
   B. The principles
      1. God has a chain of command (v. 3). The woman is subordinate, but there is a difference between that and inferiority
      2. God intended for there to be differences between man and woman (vv. 7–9). They were created differently!
      3. God wants the differences obvious (vv. 14–15)
      4. Men and women, however, are spiritually equal in the sight of God (v. 11)
   C. The practicalities
      1. Women were violating the customs of the day
         a. We don't know just how
         b. It does seem like the radical feminism of the time
      2. Paul is showing the proper relationship to custom
         a. Observe good custom (vv. 5–6)
         b. Resist wrong custom
      3. Actually, the passage does not teach about hats in church
         a. Not too sure it speaks of church services at all (cf. 14:34)
         b. Only speaking/expressing something valid to the early church. It is not a revelational cultural tenet in force today. (But we must be extremely careful in this area that we don't just write things off as "culturally irrelevant")

Conclusion:

What does the passage teach? That men and women are equal before God; that men and women are not equal in function; that the woman is subordinate to man in ministry; that such issues as hair length should not cause differences between sexes. Finally, we must evaluate the cultural/custom pressures under which we minister and find the biblical principles that apply to them.

Don't Miss the Point!

1 Corinthians 11:17–34

Introduction:

It's amazing that so many churches today want to be like the church at Corinth. The Corinthians were good, warmhearted, sincere, earnest people, but one should think carefully before any decision to replicate the pattern in Corinth. The truth is that most of both Corinthian books deal with correcting problems.

I. **The Corinthians Excesses**
    A. Detailed from 1 Corinthians alone:
        1. Confusion about human leaders
        2. Exulting in human wisdom and reason
        3. Carnality in personal, spiritual life
        4. Toleration of immorality
        5. Violation of biblical legal restraints
        6. Misunderstanding on marriage
        7. Distortion of Christian liberty
        8. Questions about separation from evil and heresy
        9. Misuse of spiritual gifts (especially in regard to tongues)
        10. Questions about the resurrection
    B. They were good people, but they had simply missed the point in a number of important areas

II. **The Communion Example**
    A. There were improper practices in connection with the Lord's Supper (vv. 17–22)
        1. Making it just an "add-on" after a church-wide potluck
        2. Creating a division between "haves" and "have-nots"
    B. There was a correction of improper practices (vv. 23–34). Paul had special revelation on this—it must have been important
        1. Details about meaning of Supper are given (vv. 23–26)
        2. Warning about misappropriation of Supper are sounded (vv. 27–30)
        3. Correction was detailed for the proper approach to the Supper (vv. 31–34): judge yourself before you come, keep the unity of the spirit, take care of your physical needs elsewhere

C. The point: this chapter is an illustration of one of the areas in which the Corinthians had missed the point

III. The Contemporary Expressions
A. Modern Christians obviously miss the point in many areas
  1. Christmas is a graphic example
  2. Finding long-term solutions in political involvement
  3. Worship (i.e., ritual, confusion, the confusion of worship with reverence)
  4. Psychological influences usually miss the point of God's provision
B. We get caught in some
  1. God wants me happy, healthy, and wealthy
  2. I've got my ticket to heaven, so I don't have to worry about the trip
  3. Something to fall back on—a safety net if things go wrong
  4. A set of options for my choice—I can choose to obey as I wish
  5. A group of components for my manipulation—I can use those aspects that fit my purposes
  6. Every one of these misses the point of Christianity
C. We need to be reminded that Christianity is not:
  1. A body of information to be known
  2. A book of rules to be kept
  3. A cluster of emotions to be felt
  4. A group of virtues to be admired
  5. A set of components to be manipulated
  6. A list of examples to be copied
D. Christianity is an expression of a life to be lived

Conclusion:
The Corinthians had missed the point on many things, and none more obvious than the Lord's Supper. We equally miss the boat on many things. God wants to do wonderful things in, with, and through us, but all too often we miss the point of what He is doing. We are careless and clueless like the Corinthians, self-willed like Israel, and indifferent like Laodicea (Rev. 3:15). Don't miss the point!

In Remembrance of Me
1 Corinthians 11:23–34

Introduction:
There is much debate regarding the Lord's Supper. What does it mean? How should it be done? How often should it be observed? Who should participate? The answers are really quite plain from the pertinent Scripture. We can say, "Paul, you weren't there." He would say, "That's right. That's why the Lord gave me special instruction."

I.   **It Is an Ordinance Not a Sacrament**
   A.   An ordinance: "something ordered or ordained"
   B.   A sacrament: "a specific means of obtaining grace"
   C.   It can't be a sacrament because
      1.   There is no grace to be obtained by the unconverted
      2.   There is no more grace to be had by the converted

II. **It Is a Picture Not a Reality**
   A.   The elements picture His body and blood
   B.   The elements do not become His body and blood
      1.   This would be a form of cannibalism
      2.   If this was intended, why did He not offer His arm?
      3.   What if it did actually become His body and blood? There is nothing more to gain, and there is nothing more to earn

III. **It Is a Celebration Not a Ceremony**
   A.   It focuses on His death
   B.   It is different from baptism which points to His death *and* resurrection
      1.   Without the resurrection, His death is pointless
      2.   Without His death, the resurrection is impossible
   C.   When we participate, we celebrate His death and all that it means

IV. **It Is an Experience Not a Routine**
   A.   It is not something to be observed by mere rote
   B.   It is designed to be a spiritual experience
      1.   It touches our minds through the exercise of memory
      2.   It touches out emotions through what is remembered
      3.   It touches our spirits through our minds and emotions

V. It Is an Examination Not an Observance
A. We do not come merely to look again at His death
B. We come to face a critical question: Was His death in vain?
C. Other questions define that question:
1. Do I have the initial right to participate?
2. Am I in a condition to participate? Am I obedient to the Lord? Am I right with other people?

Conclusion:

There are three practices of communion: *closed*—members only, *open*—anyone who wishes, and *close*—seek to limit participation by other than edict. Whatever the practice, a particular approach is advisable. Instead of saying, "You are welcome to participate," we need to say, "*Are* you welcome to participate?"

Concerning Spiritual Gifts
1 Corinthians 12:1–31

Introduction:
From a strictly exegetical and theological standpoint, the evidence to support the modern Charismatic movement is rather thin. It sometimes seems that popular practices are established and doctrines structured with inadequate regard to the Word of God. What, indeed, does the Bible say?

I. **A Basic Statement: The "tongues" in Acts and in 1 Corinthians appear to be basically the same**
    A. There are various lists of differences but not all carry much weight
    B. The insertion of the word *unknown* in 1 Corinthians 14 confuses
    C. Many can see no compelling reason to make a difference
        1. The language fits nicely
        2. Making a difference needs some clear reasons

II. **A Basic Understanding**
    According to some:
    A. Salvation and the receipt of the Holy Spirit occur at different points
        1. This view is based on Acts 19:1–7
        2. It appears, however, to miss another perfectly logical explanation of that passage and the fact that no other similar instance is recorded anywhere in Scripture.
    B. The tongues in Acts and 1 Corinthians are different
    C. Tongues are thus a sign of the reception of the Spirit

III. **Some Basic Teaching**
    A. Paul says, "Don't allow yourselves to be led astray" (vv. 1–3) (author's paraphrase)
        1. You once were very easily led off course
        2. Now you need to weigh what people say
    B. All genuine spiritual gifts are from the same source and therefore should contribute to spiritual unity (vv. 4–6; cf. vv. 12–13)
    C. Spiritual gifts are sovereignly dispensed and designed for the common good of all (vv. 7–11)
    D. God has arranged the parts of the body according to His will. Each part has a particular function and is significant (vv. 12–26)

1. Gifted people are body parts
2. Everyone has something, and everyone is designed to function
3. No one should despise or covet any gift as each has what God wills, and each is significantly important
E. No one person has all the gifts; and no one gift is for all persons (vv. 27–30)

IV. A Basic Summary
A. There is no *conclusive* evidence that tongues are different in Acts and 1 Corinthians
B. Tongues are *one* of the spiritual gifts sovereignly dispensed by God
C. Going strictly on the basis of this chapter, tongues prove absolutely nothing about anything
D. Tongues are listed last in each list, indicating that they are viewed as less important than other matters (vv. 10, 28)
E. It is clearly stated that not all have the gift of tongues (v. 30)

Conclusion:
It appears correct to say:
- Tongues are a gift rather than a sign.
- Gifts are sovereignly bestowed, not the result of some event or action.
- Not everyone has tongues (or is supposed to have them), thus ruling them out as a sign of the presence of the Spirit.
- Proper practice of gifts is much more important than the possession of them.
- Tongues should never become a matter of contention between members of the body.

The Greatest of These

1 Corinthians 13

Introduction:

This chapter is not isolated. It is part of a context. There must have been a big problem in Corinth in relation to spiritual gifts (note 12:31). The purpose of this chapter is to demonstrate that there is something far more important than gifts—namely *love*. This chapter develops the supremacy of love.

I. **The Importance of Love (vv. 1–3)**
   A. Three illustrations are given
       1. Speaking with tongues is like clashing brass or cymbals without love
       2. The very best gifts are meaningless without love
       3. Ultimate acts of self-sacrifice are of no value without love
   B. No spiritual act has meaning without love—nothing I can do is more important than love

II. **The Nature of Love (vv. 4–7)**
   A. Qualities of love listed
       1. "Suffereth long"—it is "long-minded" or patient
       2. "Kind"—disposed to be useful to others
       3. "Envieth not"—doesn't begrudge anyone anything or feel badly over anyone's prosperity
       4. "Vaunteth not itself"—does not seek to win admiration or applause
       5. "Is not puffed up"—not a mind swelled with its own importance
       6. "Doth not behave itself unseemly"—is neither rude nor crude
       7. "Seeketh not her own"—is not self-centered or selfish
       8. "Is not easily provoked"—not irritable, quick tempered, or easily angered
       9. "Thinketh no evil"—it does not keep track of evil or wrongs done
       10. "Rejoiceth not in iniquity"—is not glad about bad things that happen
       11. "Rejoiceth in the truth"—gets excited about the good
       12. "Beareth all things"—to cover with silence or to protect (based on truth)

13. "Believeth all things"—tries to put things in the best light possible (believes until there is contrary evidence)
14. "Hopeth all things"—always trusts that things will work out for the best
15. "Endureth all things"—always perseveres and hangs in against all odds

   B. Different from usual love in that these traits are
1. Nonemotional
2. Very active
3. A reasonable facsimile of the love God has for us

III. The Endurance of Love (vv. 8–12)
   A. The main point—love outlives all other spiritual gifts
1. Prophecy, tongues, knowledge will all cease
2. When? No sure answer, but surely they will end with the coming of Christ

   B. It is probably best not to try to prove that any gifts are not for today from this passage. There are better passages elsewhere
1. Note verse 8
2. Prophecy/knowledge will be abolished, and tongues will cease

IV. The Supremacy of Love (v. 13)
   A. Gifts cease but concepts continue
1. Gifts are not needed
2. The need for the concepts here are continuous

   B. Love is the greatest of all continuing concepts
1. All are recognized as great
2. If you can have only one, choose love

Conclusion:

Most of us know very little of genuine biblical love. If you are seeking gifts, be sure of love first. Our greatest spiritual need is developing love to God and showing love to others. In brief, don't concentrate on *gifts*, concentrate on *love.*

Doesn't Everybody?

1 Corinthians 14

Introduction:

Over the years, many well-meaning people have chided me about the fact that I don't have a full gospel or enjoy all that God intended for me. My response has always been to state that I have all the gospel there is and that I am fully satisfied with my spiritual life. They just sadly shake their heads and marvel at how I could be so indifferent to their claims.

I. **Examine the Claims**
   A. Some say, "I speak in tongues; everyone should"
   B. The argument is that so many things are to be found in tongues:
      1. They edify you (1 Cor. 14:4; Jude 20)
         a. Frankly, the first verse is misused
         b. The second says nothing at all about tongue speaking
      2. To speak to God divine secrets (1 Cor. 14:2)
         a. What does that verse say?
         b. It does not make the point at all
      3. To speak the wonderful works of God (Acts 2:11)
         a. This is a misuse of this passage
         b. "We hear them declaring the wonderful works of God in our own tongues [languages]!" (NIV)
      4. To magnify God (Acts 10:46)
         a. That verse doesn't say that they magnified Him in tongues
         b. "They heard them speaking in tongues and praising God." (NIV)
      5. To pray perfectly (Rom. 8:27–28)
         a. These verses says nothing about tongues
         b. It deals with the work of the Holy Spirit in prayer
      6. To give thanks well (1 Cor. 14:17)
         a. Such an interpretation distorts the meaning of the passage
         b. Actually, this section is speaking negatively of tongues
      7. To demonstrate that the Spirit bears witness with our spirits (Rom. 8:16)

        a. This verse also says nothing about tongues

        b. It actually speaks of an internal witness

   8. To know you are a joint-heir with Christ (Rom. 8:17)

        a. Again, the verse says nothing about tongues

        b. It also deals with the internal witness of the Spirit

   9. To strengthen you with might in the inner man (Eph. 3:16)

        a. Once more, the verse says nothing about tongues

        b. Again, it refers to the inner work of the Spirit

  10. To be a sign to unbelievers (1 Cor. 14:22; Mark 16:27)

        a. That is a correct use of the first verse

        b. The second passage says nothing about tongues

  11. To rest the soul (Isa. 28:11–12; 1 Cor. 14:21)

        a. That is simply not the point in the first passage

        b. The second passage contains no reference whatever to the point that is made in the claim

  12. To bring a message from God or for God to the people (when interpreted; 1 Cor. 14:5, 9, 27–28)

        a. The passage does have some reference to the claim

        b. But the claim implies something beyond the Bible

        c. It rules out any biblically nonverifiable interpretation

II. The Underlying Error of the Claim

A. Stated: the basic weakness of those who make such claims when it comes to the Bible

B. Revealed—it seems that they

   1. Feel the need of something more than the Bible

   2. Place more emphasis on experience than on the Bible

   3. Allow experience to be normative in preference to the Bible

   4. Make surface conclusions from the Bible without reference to the entirety of Scripture

   5. Go to the Bible to find support for their position rather than deriving their position from the Bible

III. **The Lessons of the Claims**
   A. Non-charismatics are not immune to some of the same errors
      1. There is much distortion and misuse
      2. There is an enormous tendency to use the Bible to prove particular positions
   B. The key to avoiding misuses of the Bible: nothing really matters other than finding out what God is actually saying or wants us to know, and that is already contained in His Word

Conclusion:

It is easy to become confused. The position of those who challenge historic orthodoxy is usually very weak because it is usually based on a very low view of the Bible. Let's be sure we build a satisfying relationship with Him based on the Bible.

The Resurrection
1 Corinthians 15

Introduction:
In the days of uncertainty in which we live, how much we need some assurances regarding eternity and the possibility of our being included in it. Such assurance is readily available to us in the Word of God, especially in this section.

I. **The Importance of the Resurrection (vv. 1–4)**
   A. It has wide prominence
      1. There is much written about it in Scripture
      2. This whole chapter is a classic location
   B. The conflict
      1. Satan and God are in unseen conflict
      2. Christ died. For Him to stay dead would be to lose the conflict
   C. The historical facts
      1. There is ample proof through witnesses
      2. In fact, it is one of the best attested facts of history

II. **The Assurance of the Resurrection (vv. 20–23)**
   A. The principle of firstfruits
      1. The Old Testament picture is clear
      2. The idea here is of one standing for all
   B. The purchase of life
      1. All deserved to die for sin
      2. As sin comes by one, so life comes by One

III. **The Method of the Resurrection (vv. 35–38, 42–44)**
   A. The illustration from nature
      1. Seed must die to grow
      2. The final product is often quite different from what has been planted
   B. The resurrection body is a different one (vv. 42–44)
      1. It is spiritual rather than physical
      2. Notice the descriptive adjectives and meanings

IV. **The Meaning of the Resurrection (vv. 54–57)**
   A. The strength of death is broken
      1. Death has lost its sting of finality
      2. The grave has no victory. It actually becomes the opening for believers to enter life

B. The only way to this victory is through the Lord Jesus Christ (v. 57)
  1. He won the victory; we must share it through Him
  2. The only way to do this is through faith in Him (John 3:16)

Conclusion:

In a day of uncertainty, it is wonderfully reassuring to know that the resurrection is one of the most well-attested facts of history. The record of 1 Corinthians makes a great contribution to this assurance, especially in this context.

Received and Delivered
1 Corinthians 15:1–11

Introduction:

The preacher of the gospel in the New Testament tradition is seen essentially as a mere conveyer of truth. We do not proclaim something new. We are not necessarily to be original (except possibly in delivery). We are charged with an adequate presentation of the message God has given to us. Paul makes much of this relationship in his ministry. The words *received* and *delivered* are used frequently.

I. **Paul Had Received and Delivered Assuredly (vv. 3–8)**
    A. The message was God-given
        1. There was no element of Paul in it
        2. He gave it absolute primacy—"first of all"
    B. The message included certain elements
        1. That Christ died for our sins
        2. That Christ was buried
        3. That He rose again the third day
    C. That message was a sure message
        1. It was "according to the scriptures"
            a. This reference is to Old Testament prophecies
            b. The death of Jesus Christ, rather than being a great tragedy, squared perfectly with the prophetic Scripture passages
        2. It was well attested by historical reality
            a. Paul's entire ministry turned upon the resurrection (he could have been instantly discredited were someone able to "produce the body")
            b. The resurrection was well proven by many witnesses: Peter (v. 5), the Twelve (v. 5), above five hundred brethren (v. 6), James (v. 7), all the apostles (v. 7), and—last of all—by Paul (v. 8) who sees himself as having been "born out of due time" in order to see Him
        3. It was amply proven in personal experience
            a. The persecutor became the preacher
            b. This is seen as due to the "grace of God," which always travels with the gospel

II. **Paul Had Received and Delivered Faithfully (vv. 1–2)**
   A. He had not changed
       1. He is speaking now of the same gospel he "had preached"
       2. He is perfectly willing for their memories to operate—one of our modern-day tragedies is that so many men "changed their minds" about the gospel
   B. He hoped that they had not changed
       1. They have received it
       2. They now stand in it
       3. They are saved by it
   C. Paul had done the job God had called him to do with absolute faithfulness—he could look back on it without shame

III. **Paul Had Received and Delivered Successfully (vv. 10–11)**
   A. The grace of God upon him was "not in vain"
       1. This means that he had genuine results in their midst
       2. He attributes this to two great sources
           a. He labored "more abundantly than you all"—he was a diligent worker for the Lord
           b. It was really the "grace of God which was with me"—we labor and the grace of God accomplishes the work. (There is nothing wrong with the grace of God. The problem must be our lack of labor in proclaiming it)
   B. Large numbers of them had believed
       1. Paul didn't care who got the credit—himself or the ones who didn't work quite as hard as he did
       2. Paul rejoiced in that men had been saved (so do we—remarks regarding improper procedure should not be designed to downgrade men or their work but to point out matters of principle)

Conclusion:
   We have been given a message: it is not our own. It is divinely given; it is absolutely attested. We have received it and are to deliver it—this is our responsibility. We are to deliver it faithfully not just in regard to the number of times we do so but also as to its contents. If we are faithful, God will give the responses in His own time and way. We are to be concerned with the faithful presentation of the contents.

If Christ Be Not Risen!

1 Corinthians 15:12–20

Introduction:

Millions of people attend church these days, but what are they hearing? In many pulpits today, the resurrection is effectively denied. Paul faced the same situation and addressed it in this passage.

I.   **If Christ Be Not Risen . . .**
   A.   Our witness is worthless
   B.   Preaching is pointless
     1.   The underlying theme of New Testament preaching was the resurrection
     2.   If Christ is not risen, preaching is merely self-help from one man to another—the divine dimension is out of it
   C.   Faith is futile
     1.   Faith comes to have identity of its own—"You gotta believe."
     2.   If Christ is not risen, there is nothing on which to hang faith, because God is a liar
   D.   Sin is sovereign
     1.   There is nothing to offer sinful man but the idea or the hope that his character may rise above it. Even if it does, however, there is the problem of guilt
     2.   If Christ is not risen, sin is sovereign, and there is no hope for guilt
   E.   Death is dominant
     1.   One gets to say more "good-byes" as one grows older, finally laying a parent, child, or mate to rest
     2.   Grief comes in the door with its message of "never again"
     3.   If Christ is not risen, then the message is "never again," and we must be drawn to the cemetery to come as close as ever we can be to our loved one
   F.   Misery is multiplied
     1.   All of these things come crashing together like a great cosmic explosion, and we are left bereft, with nothing upon which to lean or stand
     2.   If Christ be not risen, we are of all men most to be pitied—what we go through in hope of eternal life is all in vain

II. But Now Is Christ Risen from the Dead
- A. Our witness is worthwhile
    1. We speak of a living Christ
    2. We talk in terms of a living relationship
- B. Our preaching is powerful
    1. There is no substitute for it
    2. It accomplishes in spite of weaknesses
- C. Faith is foundational
    1. It is in Someone
    2. It is based squarely upon fact
- D. Sin is subjugated
    1. Bondage is broken
    2. Guilt is cared for
- E. Death is defeated
    1. Someday there will be a song in heaven
    2. "Never more" is merely the song of the raven and not the message of reality
- F. Misery is mitigated
    1. We suffer loss, pain, etc.
    2. But it is all part of a plan and for a reason

Conclusion:

If Christ is not risen—what a chamber of horrors! But He is risen, and He has become the firstfruits of them that sleep. This being so, how say some among you that He is not risen?

As God Hath Prospered
1 Corinthians 16:1–9

Introduction:

Paul is now coming to his final words in this letter. This last chapter is a bit disjointed, but it contains some items he thought important enough to include.

I. **A Collection to Be Taken (vv. 1–4)**
    A. The reason
        1. The Jerusalem Christians were in trouble
        2. It was unthinkable that early Christians should fail to help in time of need
    B. The manner
        1. To be received "the first day of the week" (an incidental Sunday observance note)
        2. Universal—"every one of you"
        3. Set aside a certain portion (with the idea of careful consideration)
        4. Based upon prosperity provided by God: this is a searching test as it shows an important, often-forgotten principle that our prosperity and our giving is related
        5. Done properly, it would eliminate pressure
    C. The destination
        1. To go to Jerusalem
        2. To be delivered by representatives of the church to insure absolute honesty
    D. Important principles spelled out here
        1. Giving should be regular
        2. Giving should be systematic
        3. Giving should be based upon principle (not according to needs or appeals)

II. **A Trip to Be Made (vv. 5–7)**
    A. Paul was going to visit Corinth
        1. Had some things to "set in order"
        2. He would do so on his way back from a trip into Macedonia
    B. He needed the help of the Corinthians
        1. It was not usually Paul's approach to rely on a specific church
        2. He needed help here so drew on a generally right principle

C. He would then spend some time in Corinth
   1. Time was needed there in accord with his usual policy
   2. Note how dependent he was upon God's will: "If the Lord permit"—we should say so, too!

III. A Work to Be Done (vv. 8–9)

A. Paul was located at Ephesus (Acts 18ff.)
   1. It was not too good a location
   2. He faced tremendous problems there
B. Paul yet saw a great opportunity
   1. An open door was there because people were there who didn't know the gospel, and he was still free to preach it
   2. "Effectual"—offering a good opportunity for success
C. There were many "adversaries"
   1. Paul read opposition differently from what we do
   2. What were and are the adversaries? People, circumstances, and lack of funds

Conclusion:

There are three critical, abiding principles in this passage:
   1. Let your giving be based on proper principles.
   2. Condition all of life by "if the Lord permit."
   3. Endeavor to read opposition properly.

"Now, in Closing Let Me Say . . ."
1 Corinthians 16:10–24

Introduction:

Paul's final word to the Corinthians appears here. Great importance attaches to the things here as they are the final summation of a great letter from a giant apostle.

I.   **The Importance of "Fellow-Laborers"**
   A.   Paul's dependence upon them
      1.   Used them widely and freely
      2.   Timothy and Apollos in view here
   B.   Paul's concern for them
      1.   Timothy was a distinct personality, somewhat younger than most, very tenderhearted, and somewhat fearful and shy
      2.   Apollos was also distinct. He had been used by the Corinthians in their party strife and likely refused to come see them for that reason
      3.   Paul was watching out for both. He tells them how to treat Timothy and shows them that Apollos is not bitter
   C.   Paul's feelings about them
      1.   They are doing the same work he is doing
      2.   He needs their support and presence
      3.   This is still a key need for the pastor today

II.   **The Importance of Christian Solidarity (vv. 13–14)**
   A.   The reasons for the commands
      1.   The evils already referred to in the book
      2.   The evils of a place like Corinth
      3.   The natural tendencies of human nature
   B.   The commandments:
      1.   "Watch ye"—be awake, vigilant, spiritually alive. This refers to making a positive effort in spiritual things
      2.   "Stand fast in the faith"—be firm in holding on to what you believe
      3.   "Quit you like men"—be brave for the faith, play the man
      4.   "Be strong"—be firm, fixed, steadfast (Eph. 6:10)

C. The underlying principle—*love*
  1. Love for Christ comes first
  2. Love for others conditions all else—Christian solidarity is a far cry from the way many of us live in the present day

III. The Importance of Christian Mutuality (vv. 15–21, 23, 24)
A. The role of respect
  1. Honor should be shown to the elders and to those who serve well
  2. We must acknowledge the contributions of others
B. The role of help
  1. Paul speaks of "laborers together"
  2. These people had supplied some lacks for him. We aren't sure just what, but their help was surely more than material
C. The role of courtesy
  1. Note the greetings brought
  2. Note the request for them to show courtesy
  3. Paul shows great personal courtesy

IV. The Importance of Knowing Christ (v. 22)
A. The centrality of Christ
  1. The book closes on this note, thus showing its importance
  2. To have or not have Christ is ultimate
B. The curse on omission
  1. *Anathema* means "eternally cursed"
  2. In this way he expressed a theological truth, a just desert, and his desire in the light of their rejection
  3. There is no excuse for missing the Savior
C. The added warning—*Maranatha*—"the Lord comes," which means:
  1. Urgency because of that coming
  2. Urgency because that coming is soon
  3. Urgency because the Lord is coming to judge

Conclusion:

These are important words here, and the most important concept of all is to see to it that one *has Jesus Christ.*